SPEAK OUT

STUDY GUIDE

MIKE BREEN

Speak Out: Study Guide
By Mike Breen

michaeljamesbreen.com
3dmpublishing.com

Cover Design: Libby Culmer
Cover Photo: Vijay Kumar, istock.com
Layout Design: Jason Zastrow

ISBN: 978-0-578-58580-2

3DM Publishing
3dmpublishing.com

CONTENTS

ABOUT THIS GUIDE

This study guide is a companion to the book S*peak Out: Awakening Mission and Discipleship through Private and Public Communication*. The goal of this guide is to provoke discussions and provide activities that help you grasp and practice the core concepts found in *Speak Out*.

While you may choose to go through this study guide on your own, I believe you will benefit most from doing it with a group. During the development of *Speak Out*, I found that people in the Huddles I was leading really started to grasp this content when they started actually trying it for themselves. Many times, one person's kairos moment helped others to really get it as well. I believe you will experience the same thing as you process what you're learning in a group.

You may choose to use this guide in a group like:

- A Huddle
- A missional community
- A house church
- A small group

- A women's Bible study
- A men's fellowship
- A youth group
- A church staff
- A college ministry
- A seminary class

The options can go on and on. Whether it's a group of two or three, or a larger group like a missional community, trying these concepts together will help everyone with the practice of cross-cultural gospel communication in whatever context God has put you in. In this study guide, we'll call any of these groups a Huddle for the sake of simplicity. Feel free to adjust the Huddle activities to account for size by dividing into smaller groups or allotting more time as necessary.

This study guide is broken up into sections. We'll refer to them as weeks, but don't feel constrained by that. If you're in a missional community that meets every other week, or in a leadership development course with monthly group check-ins, that's fine. Use the sections of this book at whatever rhythm fits your group best.

This guide will list some groups of questions as reflections. While you may choose to do these questions as discussions, we invite you to use these questions to evoke kairos moments that people in your group experienced while reading *Speak Out* or in discussion together. When someone identifies a kairos moment, feel free to pause the questions and use the Learning Circle to process the kairos moment. Don't rush

through the questions just to finish them—instead, make sure that people are taking hold of the content the book provides. If this means your group spends more time on this study guide by subdividing weeks further, that's fine.

In addition, this book will prompt your study group to do some activities found at the end of each section of *Speak Out*. Integrate these practical tools into your group rhythm as you see fit.

Try out these concepts, and I'm sure you'll find new ways to *Speak Out* and share the gospel in any cross-cultural concepts. I can't wait to see the earthquakes of awakening that happen as you and so many others *Speak Out.*

M+

COMMUNICATION
DASHBOARD

COMMUNICATION DASHBOARD

CONTENT	CONTEXT	CONVERSION
Message	History	Calling
Metanarrative	Biography	Challenge
Meme	Stance	Completion
REVELATION	**RELATIONSHIP**	**RESPONSE**

WEEK ONE

PREFACE & INTRODUCTION

REFLECTION ON COMMUNICATION

Who are some of the most effective gospel communicators you have ever heard? What do you think makes these people effective? *Note: You may choose to discuss renowned communicators or people from your personal circle.*

Which of these communicators do you think have actually sparked awakening? Explain how they did this?

In what arenas do you typically communicate with others? Which of these arenas could be avenues for gospel communication?

REFLECTION ON INITIAL VIEW OF MEMES

Put the definition for a meme in your own words.

Give an example of a meme. Why did this meme stick with you?

If the first example that comes to your mind is a meme from social media, discuss that example, and then add another example of a meme that isn't online. The fact that you remember these memes is a proof that the meme was well constructed.

REFLECTION ON AWAKENING

Why is awakening our goal as Christians?

How would you describe or define awakening?

Tell the story of your journey toward awakening. Who
contributed to this? What messages stuck with you?

CONTENT	CONTEXT	CONVERSION

WEEK TWO

CHAPTERS ONE & TWO

Chapter 1: Awakening
Chapter 2: My Gospel

REFLECTION ON INITIAL VIEW ON MESSAGE

In Chapter 1, Mike talked about what his message is. What is your first thought about what your message or your gospel is? *Note: If you haven't thought through this question before, write down the first thing that comes to mind. You can always refine this answer later.*

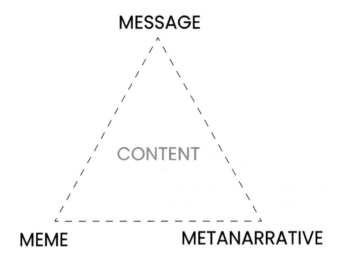

What experiences and kairos moments in your life have led you to identify your gospel?

How have you authenticated your gospel using the metanarrative of Scripture? *Give several specific examples.*

ACTIVITY: LANDSCAPE OF LIFE

In chapter 1 of Speak Out, Mike introduces the meme of the landscape of life. This meme helps us to identify the different ways we hear from God in different times of our lives.

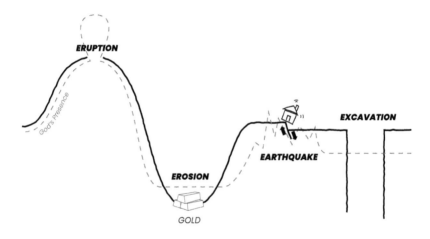

Go through the following stages of the landscape of life to identify the ways you have heard from God.

Eruptions: What have you learned during eruptive moments of God's presence?

Erosions: What have you learned from God through faithfulness in longsuffering?

Earthquakes: What have you learned from God during shocking upheavals?

Excavations: What spiritual disciplines have you developed to help you reflect and respond to eruptions?

After going through each of these four sections, answer this key question: If you were to sum up in one word or a few words what message God gave you in these parts of the landscape of life, what would it be? This is probably the heart of your message, or your gospel.

Each person should answer this question on his or her own. Then should gather in groups of three or four to process each person's journey. Processing the landscape of life should help people begin to identify

ACTIVITY: CONNECTING MESSAGE TO METANARRATIVE

Now that each person has identified his or her message, take some time to tie those messages to the metanarrative of Scripture.

What Old Testament characters and stories do you think of when you think about the characteristic of your message?

What New Testament characters and stories do you think of when you think of the characteristic of your message?

As you tie message and metanarrative together, process the particular ways that your gospel is tied to the gospel as a whole. As you can see, the starting point of each person's message is God's revelation

THE GOSPEL

My Gospel

CONTENT			CONTEXT			CONVERSION		

WEEK THREE

CHAPTERS THREE, FOUR & APPENDIX A

Chapter 3: The Tapestry of the Message and the Metanarrative
Chapter 4: The Message as Meme
Appendix A: Making Disciples through Missional Preaching

REFLECTION ON MEMES

What are some examples of memes you have heard a gospel communicator use? *This may be a preacher or pastor, but could also be from a favorite Sunday school teacher or Huddle leader. The fact that you remember these memes is a proof that the meme was well constructed.*

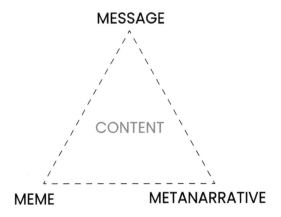

What Biblical examples of memes spring to mind?

What memes do you use when you communicate? *Give specific examples. This could be something that you use as a preacher or Huddle leader, or something you use with your kids or co-workers. Get everyone to share at least one meme that they use regularly.*

ACTIVITY: EXEMPLARS

Which of the memes your group just listed are based on examplars? Go through at least one meme example from each person and identify which ones are based on exaplars.

• Biblical examplars

• Historic or famous examplars

• Yourself

After going around the circle to analyze memes, discuss the positives and negatives of using examplars to form memes. Use this discussion to process the best ways to use examplars as memes. Go through each of the three categories of examplars during this discussion.

ACTIVITY: MAKING A MEME

Starting on Page 56 of *Speak Out*, you find concrete instructions on how to make a meme. Do this activity with your group.

You may even choose to add a week to this guide in order to give this meme-making activity the time needed for everyone to give it a go. Give them homework to prepare some memes during the week, and then analyze them together using the checklist found on page 59. It's also fine to analyze some of the memes you discussed in the reflection section above for this activity.

CONTENT   CONTEXT   CONVERSION

WEEK FOUR

CHAPTERS FIVE, SIX & SEVEN

Chapter 5: Thin Silence
Chapter 6: To Hell and Back through History
Chapter 7: Social Imagination

REFLECTION: CONTEXTUALIZATION

What is contextualization? Why is it important?

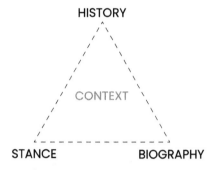

What are some of the factors that make cross-cultural contextualization difficult? How can you identify the social history of a place?

Work as a group to identify some specific, repeatable tactics.

How does metanarrative help us bridge the gap of contextualization?

List some specific ways you have seen someone connect to social history of a place to the history of God's community using metanarrative.

Why are we tempted to borrow contextualization? Why does this fail?

Have you ever tried to borrow contextualization? What happened? Why did these things happen?

REFLECTION: HISTORY AND BIOGRAPHY

How can we connect the arc of history to the biography of the people with whom we are communicating?

Re-read the Kevin Vanhoozer quote from page 85-86 of Speak Out:

> For I cannot love my neighbor unless I understand him and the cultural world he inhabits. Cultural literacy— the ability to understand patterns and products of and products of everyday life is thus an integral aspect of obeying the law of love.[1]

How does this quote link understanding biography to the Great Commission and the Great Commandment?

List some Biblical examples of how Jesus and the apostles did this.

---

1   Kevin Vanhoozer, *Everyday Theology* (Grand Rapids, MI: Baker Academic, 2007) 241.

What contexts do you need to speak out to? Look at the list on page 91, and then discuss these questions on page 93.

How do we break out of our Jerusalem and Judea?

How do we connect with the Samaritans around us?

How do we connect with the ends of the earth, even when the ends of the earth are coming to us and living as our neighbors?

ACTIVITY: SOCIAL IMAGINATION

Try out the method of connecting the Arc of History to the Crucible of Biography for the context you are communicating with.

First, identify the arc of history by answering these three questions:

What event happened?

Who were the principal characters?

Where did this happen?

Answer these questions to identify the milestones in the history of the community. Make sure you do this with all groups of people, not just the majority of an area. Keeping this focus will ensure you identify the who/what/where of events of injustice, which can be crucial in understanding the arc of history.

Now that you have a good sketch of the arc of history, begin doing interviews to draw out the crucible of biography. As you talk to people, answer similar questions:

What events have been significant in their lives?

What roles did they play in these events? Who were the other characters?

Where did these events take place?

Now that you have built the crucible of biography, tie the two arcs together as you see in Speak Out (pages 88-89) using the arcs on the following page. In your Huddle, work together on making these connections. Break into pairs or groups of three to do this. Then have each group report out to the entire Huddle. The repetition of doing and seeing together will help each person begin to understand how to use this tool.

ARC OF
HISTORY

WHAT IS THE HISTORY
OF MY COMMUNITY?

EVENTS

PEOPLE

PLACES

CRUCIBLE OF
BIOGRAPHY

WHAT ARE THE STORIES
OF THE PEOPLE WITHIN
MY COMMUNITY?

PLACES

PEOPLE

EVENTS

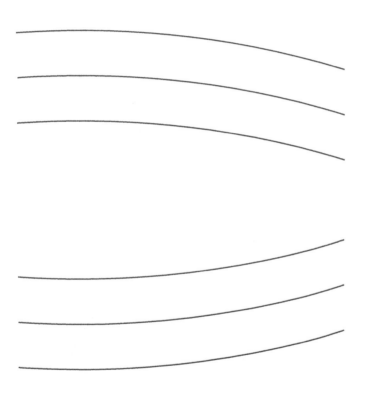

CONTENT | CONTEXT | CONVERSION

WEEK FIVE

CHAPTER EIGHT

Chapter 8: Where Do You Stand?

REFLECTION: STANCE

What is stance? Why is it important?

What kind of stances can a communicator take?

Why is it important to intentionally choose a stance?

What can communicators take stances toward?

Why is it important to nuance a stance by choosing what the stance is toward each of these things?

What did you learn about Stephen's stance in chapter 8? What kairos moments did you have while reading this?

ACTIVITY: DEFINING STANCES

Do the stance exercises starting on page 106. First, look at Paul's stance in Acts 17. Then, do the stance exercise with recent sermons or communications for each person in your group. This should be the major activity for this week; however, you may choose to spread out the stance exercise over several weeks so that everyone in your Huddle can participate.

CONTENT	CONTEXT	CONVERSION

WEEK SIX

CHAPTERS NINE & TEN

Chapter 9: The Hero's Journey
Chapter 10: The Call

REFLECTION: HERO'S JOURNEY

Describe the hero's journey in your own words.

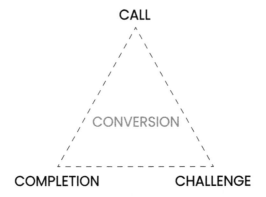

Give an example of the hero's journey that resonates with you, and discuss why it resonates.

This could be a real-life story or a hero's journey from a movie, novel, etc.

Why are all heroes broken heroes? How should we and shouldn't we let this brokenness affect our hero's journey?

REFLECTION: THE HERO'S CALL

How did you first experience the call of the hero's journey? How did this kairos moment change the trajectory of your journey?

How do we evaluate the cost of our call as heroes? Why is this a vital step of the hero's journey?

How can we communicate in such a way that we call others to the hero's journey? Why is this important? How can we use the tools we have learned in *Speak Out* to do this?

What is the difference between the call all of us experience at salvation and the particular calls we experience? Why are both important as part of our hero's journey?

How can we communicate the call to salvation effectively? How can we communicate effectively to awaken particular, personal calls? How can we use the tools we have learned in *Speak Out* to do this?

CONTENT	CONTEXT	CONVERSION

WEEK SEVEN

CHAPTERS ELEVEN, TWELVE & THIRTEEN

Chapter 11: The Challenge: Into the Valley
Chapter 12: The Challenge: Mentors and Friends
Chapter 13: The Completion of the Hero's Journey

REFLECTION: THE VALLEY

How have you experienced the valley during your hero's journey?

Create a meme that describes your time traveling through the valley on your hero's journey. Discuss how this meme can help you communicate the journey through the valley memorably.

What happens in the valley? What enemy do we face? What do we excavate? How can we communicate the valley to others effectively?

CALL

ERUPTION

God's Presence

EROSION

GOLD

CHALLENGE

How does the landscape of life fit into the challenge of the valley? How have you seen this happen in your life?

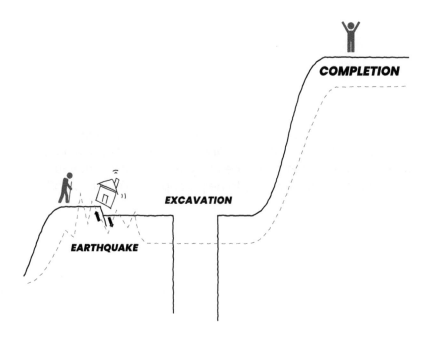

COMPLETION

EXCAVATION

EARTHQUAKE

REFLECTION: RELUCTANT HEROES

What is a reluctant hero? How have you been a reluctant hero?

How can you communicate to the reluctant hero? How can you encourage someone to move past reluctance? How can you assure people that reluctance is natural and part of the overall hero's journey?

How have you traveled the path that the reluctant hero takes— from reluctant to realistic to resolved? What personal stories can you share to communicate this journey? How can you communicate in such a way to help people travel this path?

REFLECTION: MENTORS AND FRIENDS

How do we find mentors and friends in the valley? How is the Holy Spirit the foremost of these mentors and friends?

What gives a mentor the ability to help a hero in the valley? How can we help the broken heroes around us become heroes?

How have you found mentors and friends in the valley? How can you encourage others to find mentors and friends?

REFLECTION: THE JOURNEY COMPLETE

What happens at the completion of the hero's journey? Why is this significant?

What are some examples of the bounties you have received at the end of your hero's journey? How have you shared these bounties?

What does it look like when awakening erupts? How have you seen this happen in and around you?

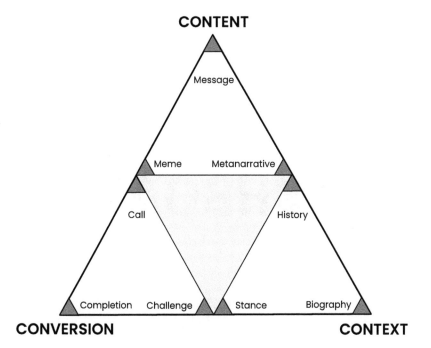

COMMUNICATION
DASHBOARD

COMMUNICATION DASHBOARD

CONTENT	CONTEXT	CONVERSION
Message	History	Calling
Metanarrative	Biography	Challenge
Meme	Stance	Completion
REVELATION	**RELATIONSHIP**	**RESPONSE**

WEEK EIGHT

CHAPTER FOURTEEN

Chapter 14: Developing a Dashboard

ACTIVITY: DASHBOARD EVALUATIONS

Use the Dashboard found in chapter 14 to review what you learned in Speak Out and in your Huddle. Then invite people in your Huddle to evaluate an upcoming sermon, seminar, or group session through this Dashboard.

You may want to break into groups of three or four to do this so that everyone has a chance to practice and to receive feedback from others. You may also choose to spend multiple weeks on this activity to ensure that everyone gets a chance to practice and receive valuable feedback from others.

IDEAS + SKETCHES

IDEAS + SKETCHES

IDEAS + SKETCHES

IDEAS + SKETCHES

IDEAS + SKETCHES

IDEAS + SKETCHES

$12.97
ISBN 978-0-578-58580-2
51297>

Lightning Source UK Ltd.
Milton Keynes UK
UKHW021941270820
368936UK00012B/327

9 780578 585802